Anatomy of a Psychotic Experience

ANATOMY OF A PSYCHOTIC EXPERIENCE

RICHARD REICHBART

IPBOOKS.net
International Psychoanalytic Books

International Psychoanalytic Books (IPBooks)
New York • http://www.IPBooks.net

Anatomy of a Psychotic Experience

Published by IPBooks, Queens, NY
Online at: www.IPBooks.net

Cover image: Ballpoint pen on smooth Bristol paper by Steven Andresen (https://www.stevenandresen.com)

ISBN: 978-1-956864-37-3

For Nansie, with all my love

Foreword

Nancy McWilliams

As I was coming of age in the 1960s and becoming increasingly fascinated with the depths of the human mind, I was strongly influenced by the writings of Theodor Reik, Freud's protégé and the first psychoanalyst with a doctorate in psychology. It was Reik's belief that "moral courage" is the quintessential requirement for being an analyst. Long before the larger psychoanalytic world came to value "not knowing" or "courting surprise" (Stern, 1996), Reik had insisted that "The courage to understand and the courage not to understand—these are not intellectual qualities, but a matter of character, an expression of moral courage, an issue of inner sincerity—manifested in spite of and often in opposition to the ego" (Reik, 1933, p. 333).

In publishing this book, Richard Reichbart exemplifies Reik's idea of moral courage. As he has commented, it is rare for a psychoanalyst to go public with an experience of significant personal psychopathology. Probably for the reasons he notes in his introduction, few analysts, either in the early days of the movement or more recently, have followed Freud's precedent and revealed their own psychological vulnerabilities. With the exceptions of Guntrip's (1975) depiction of his analyses with Winnicott and Fairbairn, and Saks's (2008) account of her own psychosis, most psychoanalytic writers have avoiding exposing their brushes with craziness, instead disguising their own mental struggles as those of a patient they once treated (Bromberg & Aron, 2019). This history makes it all the more remarkable that Dr. Reichbart has chosen to describe in harrowing detail his youthful struggle to reclaim and hang on to his precarious sanity. At the time, the psychotic condition that almost consumed him was fortunately seen as requiring intensive psychoanalytic therapy – not the medication and "management" so often (and often so glibly) prescribed today for those who fear or know they are going mad. As a beneficiary of devoted professional care that turned his life around, he has a lot to teach us.

In the small body of writing by individuals helped by talk therapy to emerge from psychotic conditions, this book is unique. The author was psychoanalytically knowledgeable even when he wrote his original reflections, and since then, his psychodynamic sophistication and specific understanding of his own psychology have widened and deepened immeasurably. I know of no other autobiographical account that includes the psychodynamically informed understanding of the affected person shortly after the period of psychosis and then decades later, when the author has added what was omitted, not fully understood, or recognized only over the years since the psychosis. In light of increasing empirical evidence that psychodynamic therapies start a healing process that continues after treatment ends, it is particularly valuable to have these reflections of a man in his seventies, whose decades of life satisfaction and productive work were launched by his earlier treatments for a psychotically fractured mind.

In this book, Dr. Reichbart simply tells his story. Following the metaphor of "anatomy," he slowly dissects his experience, leaving it to readers to consider its implications. Other than stating a wish that his account will give hope to people who suffer psychotic experiences and therapists who try to help them, he has not waxed didactic or polemical. But I can't resist doing so. There is a lot I find myself hoping that readers will take from this book. For one thing, immersion in it would be a fine way for trainees in the mental health professions to demystify psychosis and learn how psychotic problems can develop in any of us. For another, it invites readers to rethink any prior assumptions they have made, consciously or unconsciously, about the responsiveness of people in psychotic states to talk therapy. Whether or not they resonate to my own concerns, readers should know they are in for a compelling story that brings alive an era, a political context, and a set of values, speaks to the deep unconscious impact of racism even on the privileged, and provides a vivid case study in the intergenerational transmission of trauma.

Some clinicians who have heard the author speak about his experience have questioned his labeling of his youthful suffering as psychotic. Presumably, their skepticism results from their viewing the Diagnostic and Statistical Manual of the American Psychiatric Association as the "gold standard" for diagnosis; they rightly note that Dr. Reichbart's mental anguish never met DSM criteria for schizophrenia. But let me remind those who accept DSM's depiction of schizophrenia as central to their definition of psychosis that despite many decades of research, *psychiatry's failure to identify a single pathognomonic marker of what the DSM defines as schizophrenia* raises doubts about the validity of DSM criteria in defining psychotic disorders.

Even though he was not suffering a DSM-defined schizophrenic illness, it seems obvious that Dr. Reichbart was "losing his mind" in a way that cannot be understood in any other terms, and that psychotherapy helped him to keep his sanity. Most psychoanalysts understand psychosis broadly, as an extreme state of mind of varying form and content to which many of us could be subject. Dr. Reichbart struggled with paranoia, ideas of reference, concrete thinking, annihilation anxiety, hyper-reflexivity, and a profound loss of contact with consensual reality. His cognition was so disordered as to be reasonably considered delusional. These phenomena do not fit within either neurotic or borderline domains; they are consistent with longstanding observations of psychosis, starting with Eugen Bleuler's seminal work. At one time, a conclusion by the practitioner community that Dr. Reichbart had had a psychotic experience would have been automatic: as he notes, his mental state was characterized by a *fundamental distortion of reality* rather than an internal conflict from which he could take some reflective distance.

The late Bertram Karon used to joke that whenever a therapist presented a case of the successful treatment of a schizophrenic patient, some in the audience would insist that the person could not have been schizophrenic in the first place (because psychotherapy couldn't possibly "cure" a psychotic affliction). Karon (e.g., 2003) understood this protest as a primitive, group-level defense of denial against the painful realization of how badly we are failing so many people with psychotic anguish. Better to assume a diagnostic mistake than to take in the reality that the talking cure could help many patients currently consigned to medication management and a life at the margins. Better to ignore the long-term follow-up studies showing that a substantial minority of people once diagnosed with schizophrenia eventually manage to make a functional recovery without medication (see Garrett, 2019).

Many people who could go over the psychotic edge do not do so. I have often wondered how many psychotic "breaks" psychotherapy prevents – an achievement that cannot easily be empirically investigated, but one that I believe I have witnessed many times in the work of dedicated colleagues with whom I have consulted. Mental health professionals are rarely trained in psychotherapy for psychosis, partly because biological psychiatry has dominated the social construction of psychosis and partly because such training is extremely demanding. It requires not only knowledge and resources but also emotional tolerance of confusion and uncertainty, witnessing pain that cannot be quickly ameliorated, and bearing the loneliness of being the person who holds the hope. It requires moral courage.

The politics of how we think about madness has always interested me. Before 1980, the term "psychotic" was definitional of a deviation from consensual reality. Psychotic experience was viewed as at the dire endpoint of the normal-to-severely-abnormal continuum on which most human problems lie (including some problems that mainstream psychiatrists now recognize as dimensional, as in recent references to the autism spectrum, the dissociative spectrum, and the schizophrenic spectrum). Since 1980, however, our clinical concepts of "psychotic" and "psychosis" have become desiccated. At that time, several powerful groups persuaded the creators of DSM-III to frame psychological problems in categorical and descriptive terms rather than in the inferential and dimensional language that had been evolving until then among seasoned clinicians. Hence, we currently have a limited number of official psychotic diagnoses (schizophrenia, bipolar illness with psychosis, delusional disorder, schizoaffective disorder).

Pharmaceutical corporations, insurance companies, and some researchers benefit from viewing mental suffering in terms of discrete illnesses marked by present-versus-absent criteria sets (see Gnaulati, 2018). One result of their influence has been to legitimize terminology for complex psychological suffering that identifies discrete "disorders" at the expense of seeing mental problems dimensionally and assuming they have meaning. In this process, clinicians and the general public have lost a language for the kinds of distortions that happen in the more extreme versions of any psychological difficulty.

I am not the only therapist who can attest that there are many more ways to go crazy than the short list of possibilities provided by the DSM. How, for example, do we otherwise signify the critically important difference – the difference that matters for clinical understanding and treatment planning – between two hypothetical young women who meet criteria for the same DSM diagnosis of anorexia and yet have very discrepant experiences of their condition? One began restricting her eating in college but finds herself dieting too compulsively;

she goes voluntarily to the counseling center to get treatment. Her classmate, who has been limiting her food intake for as long as she can remember, was sent to counseling over her protests by friends who are alarmed that she weighs 75 lbs., is risking starvation, and yet insists she is obese. Treatment for the first patient would be significantly easier and shorter than for the second, which would require dedication, ingenuity, and probably specific interventions to save her life. In severe anorexia, there is certainly something delusional going on, as people starve themselves into physical danger while sincerely believing they are too fat.

If we use the term "psychosis" in its original meaning, denoting a break with, or deviation from, consensual notions of reality, we can see that there is a spectrum of most DSM "disorder" categories, with variants at the severe end of the continuum that often involve such breaks and deviations (cf. Kernberg, 1984; Sharp et al., 2015; Sharp & Wall, 2021). In Dr. Reichbart's case, his mental and emotional challenges centered around his identity, his core sense of who he was. In the clinical world, we have had many terms for psychotic experiences of personality disintegration, including, among many others, Bion's (1958) "attacks on linking," Frosch's (1964) "psychotic character," Winnicott's (1974) "primitive agonies," Eigen's (1986) "psychotic core," and Lucas's (2013) "psychotic wavelength."

Research on clinicians' reactions to the second edition of the *Psychodynamic Diagnostic Manual (PDM-2)* (Lingiardi & McWilliams, 2017) has shown that practicing therapists, irrespective of theoretical orientation, find it clinically valuable to conceptualize a "psychotic level" of personality organization (Gordon, 2009; Gordon & Bornstein, 2017). These broader, clinically useful understandings of psychotic experience apply to what Dr. Reichbart tries to capture in describing the dissolution of his sense of self, the shimmering new significance of specific elements of his surroundings, a feeling of basic perceptual transformation, and periods of pure terror, leading to desperate efforts to make sense of what was happening. Whatever we call this, we need to understand it better and find more articulated ways of helping people who are going through this version of hell.

The neuroleptic medications that understandably excited mental health professionals in the 1960s ushered in a long period when many of us have hoped that biological psychiatry would unlock the mysteries of psychosis, leading to increasingly effective pharmaceutical treatments that would spare us the time and expense of *listening* to people who suffer from madness. Alas, notwithstanding decades of research on the genetics, neuroanatomy, and neurochemistry of psychotic conditions, we have failed to identify a clear biological template even for DSM-diagnosed schizophrenic illnesses. Despite the fact that neuroleptics are critical for helping many people with psychotic agonies, and despite the fact that mood stabilizers are invaluable in alleviating psychotic manic and depressive expressions of bipolar illness, there is not much basis for hope that other versions of psychotic suffering, which we can delineate far less categorically, will respond to some forthcoming chemical or biological remedy.

I have known Richard Reichbart for several decades. He is a thoughtful, influential member of my psychoanalytic community and an admired analyst, therapist, supervisor, and teacher. I would never have guessed, before he wrote about his personal journey, that psychotic demons had tormented him to the degree that this compelling account portrays. In the blunter terms of a friend of his who attended his original talk at the 2012 meeting of Division of Psychoanalysis of the American Psychological Association, "I've known Richard for years, and I had no idea he was ever a nutcase!" If this book does nothing else, it should teach the lesson that there is not a categorical difference between nutcases and non-nutcases. The author remains who he was, and was becoming, when he sank into psychosis, and even at his craziest, he was always more than simply a crazy person. Like Joanne Greenberg (1964), Kay Jamison 1995), Arnhild Lauveng (2009), and others who have described healing from psychotic torment, he has been thriving for decades. Thus, the book's title aptly references not only psychosis but also creativity. I am sure that what Dr. Reichbart went through ultimately made him not only a more resilient person but also a more imaginative thinker and a more compassionate, more effective clinician.

Reading this inspiring document, I found myself wondering how many souls with similar potential, whose downward course could also have been reversed, have been ultimately lost to psychotic deterioration. Dr. Reichbart had the advantages of high intelligence and determination, but so do many others afflicted by psychosis. Without talk therapy, would he have ended up suicidal? Homeless? Incarcerated? Addicted? None of these options is unthinkable. His writing reminds us that what ultimately helps people psychologically involves humility, respect, patience, and devotion to their welfare and growth. This book could not come at a better time, when therapies of depth, insight, and relationship are under relentless assault from commercial interests determined to devalue all intensive and long-term therapeutic attachments that can bring about the kind of recovery documented here.

REFERENCES

Bion, W.R. (1959). Attacks on linking. *International Journal of Psychoanalysis, 40,* 308–315.

Bromberg, C.E. & Aron, L. (2019). Disguised autobiography as clinical case study. *Psychoanalytic Dialogues 29*(6), 695–710.

Eigen, M. (1986). *The psychotic core.* New York: Jason Aronson.

Frosch, J. (1964). The psychotic character: Clinical, psychiatric considerations. *Psychiatric Quarterly, 38*(1), 81–96.

Garrett, M. (2019). *Psychotherapy for psychosis: Integrating cognitive-behavioral and psychodynamic treatment.* New York: Guilford.

Gnaulati, E. (2018). *Saving talk therapy: How health insurers, big pharma, and slanted science are ruining good mental health care.* Boston: Beacon Press.

Gordon, R.M. (2009). Reactions to the *Psychodynamic Diagnostic Manual (PDM)* by psychodynamic, CBT, and other non-psychodynamic psychologists. *Issues in Psychoanalytic Psychiatry, 31*(1), 55–62.

—— Bornstein, R.F. (2017). Construct validity of the Psychodiagnostic Chart: A transdiagnostic measure of personality organization, personality syndromes, mental functioning, and symptomatology. *Psychoanalytic Psychology, 34*(1), 1–9.

Greenberg, J. (pseud. Hannah Green) (1964). *I never promised you a rose garden.* New York: Holt, Rinehart & Winston.

Guntrip, H. (1975). My experience of analysis with Fairbairn and Winnicott—(How complete a result does psycho-analytic therapy achieve?). *International Review of Psychoanalysis, 2,* 145–156.

Jamison, K. (1995). *An unquiet mind: A memoir of moods and madness.* New York: Alfred A. Knopf.

Karon, B.P. (2003). The tragedy of schizophrenia without psychotherapy. *Journal of the American Academy of Psychoanalysis and Dynamic Psychiatry, 32*(1), 89–118.

Kernberg, O.F. (1984). *Severe personality disorders: Psychoanalytic strategies.* New Haven, CT: Yale University Press.

Lauveng, A. (2012). *A road back from schizophrenia: A memoir.* New York: Skyhorse.

Lingiardi, V., & McWilliams, N. (Eds.) (2017). *Psychodynamic diagnostic manual, 2nd ed. (PDM-2).* New York: Guilford.

Lucas, R. (2013). *The psychotic wavelength: A psychoanalytic perspective for psychiatry.* New York: Routledge.

Reik, T. (1933). New ways in psycho-analytic technique. *International Journal of Psychoanalysis, 14,* 321–334.

Saks, E.R. (2008). *The center cannot hold: My journey through madness.* New York: Hyperion Press.

Sharp, C., Wright, A.G.C., Fowler, J.C., Frueh, B.C., Allen, J.G., Oldham, J., & Clark, L.A. (2015). The structure of personality pathology: Both general ('g') and specific ('s') factors? *Journal of Abnormal Psychology, 124*(2), 387–398.

Sharp, C., & Wall, K. (2021). DSM-5 level of personality functioning: Refocusing personality disorder on what it means to be human. *Annual Review of Clinical Psychology, 17*, 313–337.

Stern, D.B. (1996). The social construction of therapeutic action. *Psychoanalytic Inquiry 16*(2), 265–293.

Winnicott, D.W. (1974). Fear of breakdown. *International Journal of Psychoanalysis, 1*, 103–107.

Contents

Anatomy of a Psychotic Experience:

A Personal Account of Psychosis and Creativity

(H)as due recognition been given to the need for everything to be discovered afresh by every individual analyst? D.W. Winnicott

I. Introduction

Forty three years ago, before I became a psychoanalyst, I wrote a description and psychodynamic analysis of a psychotic experience followed by a psychotic break and depression which I had suffered eight to eleven years previously, that is from 1967 — 1970. It was written to fulfill a requirement for my master's thesis in psychology and also because I felt that it was important to record what had happened. It was so personal that I did not seek to publish it. It was only possible to write because at the time of the break I had gone into psychoanalysis with a particularly courageous psychoanalyst who in effect saved me. Since then, I left my previous career, got my doctorate in clinical psychology, established a private practice for adults and children, entered a second psychoanalysis, and became a training and supervising analyst. It has now occurred to me, over five decades after the experience, that I am in a better position to share the article I wrote about in the hope that I can add to our understanding of a certain type of psychotic process.

Although psychoanalytic discovery began with extensive self-revelation and self-analysis by Freud, most notably in his Interpretation of Dreams, on the whole those psychoanalysts

1

who have followed have been less inclined to reveal personal material. The determinants for this change, which may not be an entirely positive one, have been multiple, but I am sure primary among them has been a desire for professional self-protection, more in evidence as psychoanalysis solidified into an accepted profession, as well as the fear that patients who read such revelations would then experience unnecessary difficulties in the transference.

Further, it is even more unlikely that an analyst will write of anything personal approaching a psychotic experience. Such a history is usually looked upon, certainly at the time of training, as so potentially damaging as to make the individual a poor candidate for psychoanalytic training. It is true to this day that full blown psychosis usually defies psychoanalysis because reality testing is so compromised. As a result, unfortunately, gradations and subtleties that touch on the psychotic phenomenon end up not, at least for the purposes of becoming or being an analyst, being differentiated from more virulent forms of psychosis. Just the word psychotic tends to foreclose such a discussion. Further, although many analysts do write compellingly about treating psychotic patients, the history of psychoanalysis from Freud onward is replete with analysts issuing the ultimate attack upon another analyst to discredit him: that he is psychotic. Thus, particularly in this instance, as so often happens in the psychoanalytic profession, there is not very secure ground to speak openly about one's personal experience.

And of course there is an added and even practical concern: we tend to practice with secrecy about ourselves, with non-disclosure, on the understandable grounds that to speak too much of oneself will affect our patients and color in some way the transference or even discourage a patient from choosing one as an analyst. Of course, there are debates about this when it comes to the immediate clinical work, some analysts and some theories contending that self-disclosure can be helpful, even necessary, to the patient to explain an interaction between patient and analyst. But even here it is unlikely that the analyst will publish a revealing personal history involving emotional difficulties, even though those difficulties have passed.

I have chosen to present this material in an atypical fashion by first sharing what I wrote back then, virtually unchanged, and then by making some comments about it. This is the only way I can think to provide a sense of immediacy to what I experienced. It also has the virtue of presenting in one place three ways in which I have processed these events: at the time of the events themselves, the academic article written eight to eleven years later, and my thoughts now fifty years afterward looking back on the experience.

The experience, powerful as it was and potentially permanently disabling had I not received in a timely fashion effective psychoanalytic treatment, did not involve any hallucinatory manifestations nor any obvious compromise of what we commonly call "reality testing", although there were at times feelings of paranoia. Nevertheless, self-protectively back then when I wrote up this experience, I left out some material to minimize the extent to which I was affected by the psychotic break as well as the depression which followed the psychotic experience. For one, I left out that at the time of the break, prior to entering psychoanalysis, I had voluntarily entered an inpatient psychiatric facility (as I recall for three weeks) because I was so unable to stay calm. The effect of being in this setting was to slow me down, with tranquilizing medication and through visits by the psychiatrist who admitted me with whom I could converse, sufficiently so that I could focus on what my next step should be. I realized instinctively that I could not get enduring help in a hospital group setting, to which I adjusted only too readily. Fortunately my psychiatrist — not a psychoanalyst himself — urged me to seek out a psychoanalyst in a larger city, none being available locally, for in-depth work as soon as possible. So I left the inpatient facility to drive alone a considerable distance to find accommodations in a different city where I had an appointment, and where I had a few friends and distant family members, and thus began my psychoanalysis.

For another, the extent of my on-coming depression after the break was longer, grimmer and more paranoid than I state in the article, although I was able to function. And lastly, my psychoanalysis was actually briefer in time than mentioned in the article and was more in the nature of a transference cure, something which I sensed but could not entirely articulate at the time. It was not until my second psychoanalysis — many years later — that I more fully integrated the dynamics discussed here. I will expand on these points further on.

Lastly, I was wonderfully happy and productive for a period of time that was bound, unbeknownst to me, to come to an end as will be seen. During that time, no one — including myself — would have thought there was anything wrong, which is very different than many other psychotic episodes. But let me tell the story.

What follows is the article written in 1978.

II. The Article

This article recounts a psychotic experience occurring to me which lasted approximately one year (in its functional stage) and some of the events which preceded and followed it. I attempt to give a subjective view of what the experience was like and a psychoanalytic appraisal of the dynamics of the experience. Of course it is impossible for any article to do full justice to the interrelated and varied material of daily life, no matter what the mental state of the individual involved; and this particular material is taken largely from my memory of events which occurred eight to eleven years ago (from approximately 1967 to 1970) during which time I did not keep records. Thus, this article captures, as if through a time-distorted glass, the events as they were experienced and even then does so selectively, based on what appears important in the present.

In many ways this was an experience "encapsulated" in time: It had a precipitating event or events and was ultimately followed by a psychotic break of large proportions. At the beginning of the experience, and even more so at the end, I was aware of a change in my personality; but in the beginning the change was interpreted as a triumphal one and only in the end, when further distressing transformations began to take place, was I aware that something was seriously amiss. The experience, which took place roughly between my twenty fifth and twenty seventh years, was followed by psychoanalysis of roughly three years, with a break at one point, and more or less successful termination at that juncture.. For the sake of clarity, I have divided the psychotic experience into five stages, which I call precipitating, transitional, functional, disintegrating, and psychotic break.

I have attempted to describe some of the manifest aspects of my personality during each stage, the subjective experience in each stage which in many instances resembled an altered state of consciousness, and the psychological logic of the stages. This psychosis did not involve any hallucinations nor was it at all obvious to others during its functional stage. On the contrary, whereas during the beginning and final stages it was clear that something was wrong, during the functional stage I exhibited little manifest impairment and had minimal difficulty in reality testing. I did not suffer amnesia for these events, although memories for past personal history, that is for events prior to the psychosis, underwent dramatic rearrangement during the psychosis in terms of their immediacy of recall and their significance to me. In fact, this last characteristic — the rearranging of past memories as if one were reshaping one's history out of the same basic plastic material — was one of the important data of the experience. The fact that this restructured history, and the necessarily accompanying personality, was on its most fundamental level constructed on incorrect concepts was not something I realized until the entire structure began to crumble toward the end of the experience.

Adult psychoses, of varying degrees of severity (often considerably more severe than mine was) have been analyzed in the literature since Freud (e.g. Freud, 1911, 1924a, 1924b); and have been described from the subjective viewpoint (e.g. Macalpine & Hunger, 1955; Bowers, 1974), although with considerably less frequency. Why then another account? One of the characteristics of the literature concerning psychosis appears to me to be the inability to combine in one account the subjective aspects of the experience with an analytic understanding of what is happening. The subjective experience — particularly the altered state aspect of it — is of tremendous power (to judge from my case and other reports), shot through with valid insights despite the serious nature of the illness. Personal accounts often stress this aspect of the experience without beginning to penetrate to analytic understanding of the transformation. On the other hand, analytic accounts are all too often devoid of any appreciation of the often accurate insights and the very powerful altered state which accompanies the psychotic experience, at least in its less virulent forms. Perhaps one of the reasons for the inability to combine analytic insight with subjective appreciation of psychosis is that the combination in one recovered individual exists infrequently; or — as psychosis still retains a pejorative ring in professional circles and psychoanalysts on the whole are considerably more reluctant than their founder to offer self-analysis for public scrutiny — those in a position are not inclined to write about themselves. Regardless, I hope that by this account I can portray both the feel and the logic of a psychotic episode.

The Background: Separation Trauma and Oscillatory Patterns

Some background is necessary to suggest that the psychotic episode, far from being cataclysmic, was the natural culmination of a process which (at least in the wisdom engendered by hindsight) had been building for a long period. This is not to imply that there was any obvious difficulty in my psychological adjustment during my early years. On the contrary, from outward appearances my adjustment throughout adolescence was deceptively good. However, beneath the surface, lay a combination of troubling factors, whose roots could be traced to early childhood; and the most important of these factors was separation trauma in the establishment of object relationships.

I was born in 1943 in upstate New York, the only child of Jewish parents. During my first two years, I lived almost exclusively in the Adirondack resident of my maternal grandparents with my mother while my father was stationed in the Army at Camp Kilmer, New Jersey. My mother — an intelligent, attractive and often sensitive woman — had no tolerance for the frustrations of daily living. Given to fits of impatience and depression, frequently marked by poor health, she tended to withdraw from the demands of reality into the world of literature and poetry. Her favored defense (and aggression) was to read compulsively regardless of the exigencies of the moment. As a consequence, control over daily life often fell by default to others, in the immediate family setting particularly her own mother under whose manipulative power my mother waged a constant but largely ineffectual rebellion. The sometimes uncertain attention of my mother and the absence of my father led to my establishment of strong object relationships with my maternal grandparents.

My grandfather, upon whom my mother apparently modeled at a young age many of her good and bad traits, was a country doctor of considerable Old World charm. He had a delightful, teasing sense of humor and a sensitive grasp of personality; but he too was given to fits of impatience (often explosive in quality) and periods of depression in which, by reading or some similar method, he would withdraw into himself. In addition, he could at times prove dictatorial and impatiently cruel. Toward him, I developed an intense sense of attachment and identification; and in turn, he was extremely fond of me as his first grandchild. My grandmother —- toward whom I was also very attached — was a character out of a different mold: Possessed of an immense drive, she had, with limited family resources and family educational background, graduated from Columbia School of Dentistry, become a practicing dentist (which helped to finance my grandfather's medical training; he had previously assisted her through dental school through his work as a watchmaker), raised three children, and managed the family home. She possessed an optimistic, social turn of mind, as contrasted to my grandfather's frequent pessimism and misanthropy; but — as might be expected — she could be highly and skillfully manipulative. Together, my grandparents fashioned a secure and comfortable home (which also served as their offices) in which as an infant and child I received a great deal of attention. The importance of this country home set in a picturesque town in the midst of beautiful Adirondack countryside to my psychological development became clear in the dynamics of my subsequent psychosis.

My father had been raised entirely in New York City. He shared many of my grandmother's qualities: He too was possessed of an exceptional drive and of a social and optimistic character. Although his family had been comfortable, his father died unexpectedly when he was eight; and the family (his mother, his sister and himself) had suffered a severe change in fortune. He had managed to become an attorney, but at the time of my birth he was still relatively poor. Highly manipulative, he denied his aggression toward those closest to him but beneath this surface lay a sense of terrible rage, which sometimes expressed itself by days of silence directed toward the offending party. When I was a child, my father appeared like an intruder into the family setting, coming and going infrequently as dictated by his duties in the service. Of these times, I retained little subsequent awareness (until analysis). When I was approximately four, my father was released from the service, and my mother, my father and I settled in New York City. Here my father became the central figure in my struggle to mature. Through me as his only child, he lived part of his struggle to succeed (and to regain the family comfort which he had lost when a child), exhibiting an obsessive need to design my career and control my accomplishments. As a result, in childhood I became an achiever in a variety of areas, but — as the years progressed — my accomplishments were not sufficient to entirely assuage his (or my now introjected) needs. To complicate matters, due to his compulsive work habits, my father was infrequently at home. As much as I tried to rebel against the controlling aspects of this relationship (the overprotective manipulation combined with the infrequent presence), there was little actual rebellion throughout my high school and college career and a great deal of ambivalent worship of my father and reliance upon his judgment and largesse. But the contrast between the setting in New York City, both physical and psychological, and that of my grandparent's country home was becoming subtly but progressively a part of a developing oscillatory pattern in my personality.

I have tried, so far to unfold the background information descriptively, only hinting at psychoanalytic dynamics, so that one can achieve a sense of development in the manner of a mystery story, which is how — to some extent — the events were lived by me. For I wish to stress that in growing up, I (and those around me) had no awareness of developing mental illness. I knew that I was a sometimes frenetic, determined sort of character; but the extent to which I excelled, which happened with a consistency which surprised me, and which earned the approval of my father, blinded me to the difficulties in my relationship to others and in understanding myself. There were revealing discomforts, however, many of which centered upon my relationship to my father: I could be excessively shy, but usually attempted to disguise my shyness with bravado; I imitated my father's manner consciously; I became increasingly calculating in seeking acceptance from others, carefully planning, for example, to win popularity contests in school or summer camp and succeeding without revealing my intention;

14

I tried to adapt my character to situations at hand and was adept as well, at playacting in school and camp productions; I frequently distanced myself from situations in which I felt humiliated, powerless or upset by thinking of myself as a young novelist who would subsequently write of just such a situation in a brilliant style reminiscent of Faulkner, Melville or Joyce; I did not seem able to join in typical adolescent rebellions or criticisms of authority near at hand; I seemed only able to succeed in goals approved by my father; and at the same time I felt suffocated by my father's attentions. I remember one instance in particular which I felt at the time representative of my plight and especially humiliating: I had decided to leave home for the summer by shipping on a freighter, but I found to my chagrin that I needed my father's assistance to leave home in this manner, for he could get me into the seaman's union. Thus I found myself one day at the union headquarters, surrounded by assorted varieties of crusty seamen, being shepherded by my father to the official with whom he had some influence and being kissed by my father (he continued to caress and kiss me beyond the stage where in our culture it was generally accepted) in this setting. With that kiss, my romantic dreams of going to sea, for which I was ill prepared anyway, died a painful death. In effect, what I wanted from my father was his permission to rebel and his protection in the process.

None of these symptoms was unusual in an adolescent, except that my sometimes desperate wish to escape the strictures of my family setting increasingly became part of the oscillatory pattern in my personality which developed when I attended Yale College. The established, stuffy setting of this institution, one chosen for me by my father, proved a further aggravation of my growing tendency to avoid close peer relationships and to imitate gentlemanly characteristics of my father, whose father-image air was especially well defined. During these years, I compulsively studied as a premedical student with the hope of following in my grandfather's footsteps, isolating myself from companionship and attempting to overcome my shyness by a hale-fellow-well-met-attitude when I did venture forth . I was neurotically competitive: as I succeeded in my studies, I failed in the continuous, integral development of my character. But during my summer vacations, a transformation occurred: escaping the Yale environs, I indulged in a variety of formerly repressed interests in writing and art, established often intense peer and tentative sexual relationships, expressed excitement and romanticism often in conjunction with country settings, and usually exhausted myself in the process. Then, as suddenly, in returning to school in the fall, I cruelly cut my summer friends by failing to communicate with them and returned to my lonely, gentlemanly pursuits. This oscillatory aspect of my personality was more marked than could be expected from the circumstances of summer vacation itself, although at the time I did not find it unusual.

This oscillatory pattern came to a head once before the event which finally precipitated my psychosis. When I graduated from Yale College, I spent a chaotic time; and the development of the psychosis was probably temporarily stayed by my return to the same academic environment a year later. As Bowers (1974) has documented in his studies of emerging psychosis, graduation for college or graduate students tends to ignite latent psychoses. The dependency and routine of the academic setting may become a haven for the student with a poorly integrated ego; and this haven is threatened by graduation and the transition from student to "civilian" status. Certainly, this was the case with me: when I graduated from college, I spent a year in which I increasingly sensed (but beneath the surface of conscious articulation) that unless I returned to the familiar (if psychologically uncomfortable) academic setting and routine from which I had fled, my personality would undergo a disintegration. In effect, my ego had established a fragile stability dependent upon an association to a particular place and a particular role; it could not make a successful transition outside this protective environment.

Graduation was presaged by a crucial decision in my senior year: I decided, after having completed my required premedical studies, not to apply to medical school, and therefore not to follow in my grandfather's footsteps. The reasons for this decision were various, the most significant to me at the time being that I felt my talents lay more in the humanities than in the sciences; but the most important reasons lay beneath the surface of my consciousness. Instead, without any previously expressed interest, and without any courses that would indicate such an interest, I decided to apply to law school. At graduation, where as class orator I delivered the commencement address (unrelated to grades: I had won a contest for class orator), I was expected to enter Harvard Law School in the fall.

It was not to be. Freed now from the strictures of the Ivy League, and what Yale College had represented to me, I spent the next year in a frenzied rebellion, a desperate attempt to throw off the chains I felt bound me. At the last minute, enlisting the surreptitious aid of a playwright friend of my parents, I gained admittance to the University of California at Berkeley as a graduate student in playwriting; persuaded my parents to finance my education there instead; and arrived in the unrestricted atmosphere of Berkeley in the fall of 1964 — a far cry at the time from the hallowed, conservative halls of Yale. Here at Berkeley I tried my hand at acting and playwriting; and then I became involved in the student movement at the University — the Free Speech Movement — being arrested in Sproul Hall for "sitting in" with 800 other students. In this new environment, I felt as if I were released and blossoming. But

I had neglected to concentrate on my courses; and to prevent poor grades from being entered on my record, I simply dropped out of school. Just as simply, the Selective Service board threatened in kind to drop me out of my student deferment status. I did not wish to be drafted nor serve in the Vietnam War; and so — scurrying around to find graduate schools to enter — I enrolled (just in time) at the University of Minnesota graduate program, this time in the English department. Here, however, in an atmosphere which was also a far cry from Yale, I once again became involved in political activity: I helped to organize a group of Minnesota students for Martin Luther King's Southern Christian Leadership Conference and with money collected from the Minneapolis-St. Paul community, we spent the summer in a small Southern town in Peach County, Georgia, organizing Blacks and registering Black voters. I found the experience exhilarating and emotional, enjoying immensely my responsibilities, and identifying with the Blacks there. I lived with a Black family in this town; was joined by my girl friend at the time from the East; and thought I was thriving in the experience. Near the end of the summer, I decided to return to Yale, this time to attend law school there . . . and so, cruelly cutting my girl friend and my other friends, I reentered the safe academic setting where I had been so miserable (but so secure) for four years. In effect, I grasped for the only reed I recognized, after a year adrift in a sea of new, unstructured and often rebellious experiences. It should have been apparent to me that I could not swim, but I did everything to keep that knowledge from myself. Instead I attempted to integrate these experiences into a contrived, respectable ego: I saw it as a logical, if unusual pattern for an emerging young Yale lawyer interested in civil rights. I was determined now to hold things together by fashioning myself into this image. In fact, I had only succeeded in delaying the inevitable.

Approximately two years later, I had succeeded in achieving part of this goal: I had not undergone as marked oscillations. What was happening was that my emotional life was being rigidly repressed; I was more and more losing my emotional and response flexibility by forcing myself into the lawyerly mold I had chosen. At the same time, my sense of rebellion was on the verge of shattering the sanctity of the Yale halls themselves; I had become head of a Student Committee to urge reforms in the grading and administrative procedures at the law school. Lastly, sensing that I was terribly at a loss emotionally, I had tried to find in a female law student from New York University a bulwark against the encroaching lack of sensation I seemed to be experiencing. It was at this time that the precipitation event of my psychosis occurred: my grandfather died.

Stage One: Precipitating State

The last time I saw my grandfather , a time which became invested with especial significance to me during my psychosis, was in a hospital room at the University of Vermont College of Medicine in Burlington. I had driven to Vermont in haste from New Haven with my girl friend when I discovered that my grandfather was to undergo an exploratory operation for an internal difficult which had been giving him pain for years but which he had delayed having treated. I found him fully functional, in good spirits, but exhibiting marked swelling of the feet. I introduced him to my girl friend. She was the only girl friend I had ever introduced to him (although he had known a previous one from his country town); and I viewed the introduction as a kind of benediction for her. Two aspects of our subsequent conversation stayed with me: in one, my grandfather wanted to know what the time was. I had no wrist watch and said so; and my grandmother mentioned in passing that none of the clocks in their home seemed to be working properly. To ascertain the time, we had to look out the window at a clock tower on campus. In the second, my grandmother discussed how my grandfather had spent the day prior to his leaving for the hospital in saying goodbye to all his old friends in their country town; it seemed as if he were carefully preparing for his death. We left two days before the exploratory was to take place. He died the day after the operation at the age of 79: the exploratory had revealed cancer of the liver.

A few days after his death, I received a package in the mail: I immediately knew by its size and hospital return address what it contained. Unknown to me, after we had left him, my grandfather had insisted that my grandmother immediately purchase for me a wristwatch and send it to me. I cried when I opened the package, and the entire incident with its evident symbolic significance, as well as the hospital visit itself, became highly cathected for me. Shortly thereafter, I proposed to the woman law student and we became affianced.

I was not aware of it, but I had experienced the event which was to precipitate the psychosis.

Stage Two: Transitional Stage

Progressively, for a period of approximately ten months, I underwent a personality change, at first not obvious to me and then unavoidably so. I found myself more and more disenchanted with my choice of career and with myself for making that choice. It seemed as if, with my grandfather's death, I realized how far I had strayed from my inner beliefs which I associated to him; how barren, from an emotionally satisfying point of view. the legal profession was for me as compared to the other option which I had foregone, namely medicine; how ridiculous were the legal sophistries with which the profession attempted to disguise the true import of actions; and how dismal city life was — despite its compensations — when compared to the country life which I associated with my grandfather. Circumstances made these beliefs, most of which I associated with my grandfather's misanthropy, his disdain for city life, and his choice of a career in the country, easy to sustain for it was now the height of the Vietnam War crisis: Freshman law students no longer had guaranteed deferments and were sweating out the lottery, while seniors were either thankful that they would be 26 (the magic age) at graduation and not draftable, or — like me — were considering how to avoid the draft between the time of graduation and their twenty-sixth birthdays. One of the elective courses I was taking involved the students in the pioneer work of creating a Selective Service Law Reporter, designed to bring Selective Service law into its own and stop the bureaucratic dinosaur from its frequent violations of its own statutes and regulations. And, in the midst of the school year, with the national election campaign in full swing, the assassinations of Robert Kennedy and Martin Luther King occurred. It was not exactly a time in which the most rational of men would be unswayed in his faith in civilization.

I put myself, as head of the student committee, in the midst of this crisis, challenging the law school to take a stronger stand against the Vietnam War, advocating a revised grading system (which was subsequently adopted after I graduated), and questioning the administrations use of some of its funds. For the first time, I was carrying my sense of rebellion into an arena which represented for me my father. As I did so, however, I became increasingly more frenetic, increasingly depressed about my presence at school. I found, in my attempt to single-handedly do so much, that I was having difficulty concentrating, completing projects, and in particularly reading legal works or writing in legal terms. At the end of school, my final grades were extremely poor and for the first time in my school career, I failed a course. My difficulty in functioning had become marked by then; I forced myself to re-do a paper for the course, this time revealingly on "Gun Control", but it was sheer agony for me to read and to put together the meaning of words. I knew now that something was seriously wrong.

But I was determined to successfully fight through the situation on my own; and in doing so, I felt that I had to oppose a variety of forces. For one, I had succeeded in getting a position for myself and my fiancée in a legal services program on the Navajo Indian Reservation in Arizona and New Mexico (through a fellowship from the University of Pennsylvania). The job was almost a guaranteed draft deferment. But my father wanted me to take, instead, a considerably better paying job in Manhattan; one which promised no guarantee of a deferment. I saw this situation in somewhat lucid terms as my father's need to maintain control over me at *all* costs. In addition, Yale Law School threatened me (I had become thoroughly obnoxious to them by then) with the prospect of re-doing an entire *year*, something which was both ridiculous and impossible — the Selective Service would have snatched me away to begin with. (The school ultimately backed down, but not until October of the fall term.) Lastly, I went to an analyst in New York City, but his desire to put me into an institution — he no doubt correctly assessed what was happening — was something which I would not abide. I felt, in fact, that as difficult as the time I was having, I was on my way to a necessary breaking of my dependency on my parents and to a final breaking from New York City which I perceived as a place certainly as insane in its neuroticism as anything I could dream up on my own. (The analyst's attempt to convince me of New York's relative sanity was one of the deciding features in my decision not to remain.) In addition, I felt that I had to make my personal statement about the Vietnam War, and helping the Navajo Indians seemed to me as symbolic a gesture as any, at a time the country was determined to kill the natives of a foreign land.

However, whatever the tenor of my ostensible motives, whatever their virtue, the fact was that psychologically I was going through extreme change. I found it impossible to be with my fiancée, and — although she attempted to help me in my evident psychological distress — I felt that I had to leave her; and this despite my feelings of the significance of her introduction to my grandfather. In shaky condition, I went by myself to the training program in Philadelphia for new attorneys for legal services organizations; and I found that I could not comprehend the legal aspects of the program (much of which, in addition, was irrelevant to the Navajo reservation). However, my senses were gradually becoming more "acute": I felt compelled to get into the country. I drove out to Lancaster county, an area of rolling hills and fertile farms, and here — away from the hurly-burly of the cities which I had come to despise so much since my grandfather's death — I seemed to find rest for my oversensitive senses. I experienced a sense of awe and peace in the presence of trees, grasses, streams, and hillsides; enjoyed sleeping under the stars; and felt the washing away of my anxiety. In effect, what I was experiencing was that "oceanic feeling," that altered state of consciousness, characteristic of the psychosis. More than anything else, it was the pure beauty which I experienced, which made me so grateful that it brought tears to my eyes. I tried my hand, without much success, at picking peaches and tobacco at some local farms; and then my training program in Philadelphia was over, and it was time for me to depart for the Navajo reservation.

Stage Three: Functional Stage

My situation on the Navajo reservation was certainly ideal for the nurturance of my psychosis. The reservation is an open and isolated spot, 25,000 square miles in extent, about the size of the state of West Virginia; a spot marked by a subtle, often austere, and breathtaking beauty: a semi-arid expanse, broken by washes and gullies, and large, sensuous sandstone formations, in which the play of different textures and different pastel shades and the changes in the light are endlessly exciting. Here I found a feeling of joy, a kind of slowing down of time and widening up of perception, so that observing the play of light on a small stream and listening to the sound of the water was a mystical experience.

Not only did the natural world seem more vividly observed, but I found I was more certain of my creative instincts: I wrote poetry (much more than I had during the later period of my neurotic personality) without hesitation, as if it came bubbling from within; I drew pictures without a need to correct; and I felt as if I could formulate concepts about individuals I met, and their lives, in terms more certain than I could have before. In addition, I seemed to be able to hear music in a manner which I had not been able to before, knowing instinctively what I liked and why I liked it; and what I heard as "false" and not "from the heart". (My taste tended to run toward single vocalists such as Bob Dylan, Leonard Cohen, Tim Buckley, Joan Mitchell, Joan Baez and Edith Piaf — who spoke about the loneliness of life, which I found especially moving at the time.) I had never placed much importance upon music before but now, for the first time (one of my first pay checks went to the buying of a stereo system) I had records in my home which I played repeatedly.

Further, I found myself placing more symbolic importance upon events which took place and upon people's actions. I was aware, for example, in a way that I had not been before, how much people's actions characterized their lives or represented a broader statement than they intended. There was nothing psychoanalytic about this perception, but it was all pervasive. In particular, I thought of my own actions in this light; and more and more I found myself comparing my actions to those of my grandfather. I was emulating my grandfather's life: leaving my "native land" (he had emigrated from Russia at a young age) and my family for a distant, better country. I seemed to look upon life, and people in a manner similar to his and with a certainty which reminded me of him: I was very positive when I thought I saw people's motivations. In fact what I was experiencing was that "sense of certainty" and relief from anxiety which so characterizes the psychosis: I was very much unaware of ambivalence in myself although I believed I could see it in others.

My job on the Navajo reservation was also ideal for the nurturance of my psychosis: I worked efficiently (up to a point . . . I had difficulty achieving closure on my work); and I had little difficulty negotiating the personality interactions attendant upon my job. But the job itself represented an extremely rebellious one as far as my culture was concerned: We were a small enclave of young lawyers and Navajos, with monies provided by the Office of Economic Affairs, suing and legally opposing all the "establishment" powers — the Bureau of Indian Affairs, the merchants in the surrounding white communities, the Department of Interior, the traders on the hundreds of trading posts which economically controlled the reservation, even the Navajo Tribal Government itself (which was reluctant to enforce the Indian Civil Rights Act which had recently been passed). This position then fit very much the needs of the psychosis to create a world of its own.

Eventually, I befriended Darlene, a Navajo woman, with a child of four years. I had, in the process of settling on the reservation, befriended other women, and fairly brutally dropped them. But Darlene, who was from a very poor background but had managed to achieve a college education, was bright, determined and a reminder for me of the kind of determination represented by my maternal grandmother. It was the first really intimate contact in which I felt I had an investment since my successful emergence from the East, and

I was determined to make it last. I found myself uncritically in love. Without knowing it, (again!) I was beginning a process which was to lead to the disintegration of the psychosis.

Stage Four: Disintegrating Stage

The relationship with Darlene, who was — revealingly enough — a preschool teacher (as well as the founder of a Navajo youth group dedicated to challenging the established structures on the reservation), had all the romanticism and beauty inherent in my often altered state of consciousness. I also found that I identified very much with her four year old girl, that I felt that I could understand intuitively her feelings and ways of processing and struggling with information. But increasingly spurred on I felt by Darlene, I found myself within my organization taking more extreme positions — the organization itself was a frequent meeting place for young Navajos interested in opposing the often repressive institutions on and around the reservation. As I did so, I increasingly came in conflict with the head of the organization, and thus I became a rebel in a rebel camp. I therefore moved out of the main office to the office run by an intelligent and very neurotic lawyer who reminded me very much of my grandfather. I was now away from the main office (located in Window Rock) in an isolated office (in Crown Point,

New Mexico) where my Navajo girl friend frequently joined me. The closer the end of my fellowship came, the more difficulty I got into with the head of the organization; and I began to feel an increasing sense of paranoia in reference to him. I was becoming a scapegoat in the organization; and at the same time, I found that I was ambivalently pushing Darlene toward my newly acquired lawyer friend. Further, I was increasingly having difficulty in concentrating again, traveling frenetically within the vast expanses of the reservation to handle cases in the field.

What was happening was that at the point which it seemed logical to make a commitment, to take a next step, in my relationship with the Darlene by marrying her, I was unable to "move" psychologically. The reservation and the job were so highly cathected for me that it was impossible for me to shift the scene. In addition, Darlene, so embedded in the Navajo culture yet at the same time so reminiscent for me of my grandmother, was a mother figure. One of the last poems I wrote to her (and the only one which I retain) at a time I sensed that our relationship was in the process of disintegration, read:

Teach me
How to touch your skin
And feel it in my fingertips
How to know your hair

Across my face
And your whisper in my ear
For I have forgotten,
Forgotten the sand beneath my toes,
The mist hanging in the trees.
The smell of wet wood.
When I was a child,
I knew the raindrops, the sand, the wet wood,
And I would be a child again,
If you would teach me.

The poem was dated almost two years, to the day, from my grandfather's death. It was sometime thereafter that I wrote my last poem in which I recounted a particularly vivid experience: I had been walking through a grove of trees, when I seemed to see myself as an old man with white hair, and had a sense of the passage of time which I had not experienced before. This was perhaps the closest I came to losing, for a moment, the distinction between myself and my grandfather. In a sense, it was an announcement that the drama was about to end.

From here, the disintegration of the psychosis continued quite rapidly: my year of employment was over and I had located a job with a well-known legal services organization in California. I left to secure the job and supposedly to bring Darlene and her child with me, but when I arrived in

California, I was having difficulty making decisions and also increasing difficulty simply in being physically in one place. I located one job, tried it out, dropped it, located another, tried it out but could not concentrate; even had located a house for us to live in — but by this time I had kind of a "bald-eyed" look; and I was visibly disturbed. I finally returned to the reservation only to find that Darlene had gotten tired of waiting and tired of my uncertainties, and found another (whom she subsequently married).

Stage Five: Psychotic Break

Now the disintegration was in earnest: I found that "sense of light" which had characterized the psychosis gradually receding; and I no longer knew quite what my personality was or how to function. When I read, I had difficulty knowing how to view the words, for I tended to look at them through my "introjected" perception of what Darlene would think on reading the words. I found writing equally difficult. And my physical movements were uncertain because I did not, increasingly, know exactly how to do the most mundane things. In addition, the responses of which I had been capable in the psychosis, the apparent breadth of the responses, was fast diminishing: I was entering a depressive, paranoid state (incidentally with a tremendous feeling of head pressure — not really comparable to a headache but continuous). At one point, I smoked marijuana (I seemed to become interested in marijuana as the psychosis disintegrated — I had never been interested before — as if I wished to magically retain the psychotic experience) and became terrified when I found that I spoke the way I had, years ago, in New York City — with a more pronounced New York accent and Jewish idioms. I knew now that the sense of triumph when I had obtained my "psychotic freedom" had been premature: I was in trouble. Through a series of circumstances, I finally managed to arrive in Denver at the doorstep of a well-known psychoanalyst, who — as soon as he saw me (I managed to maintain good control over my "telephone voice" so he had no inkling) and my inability to stay still — said, "You're at the ragged edge". Over a period of four and a half years, beginning with seven-day- a-week- therapy, (and involving a brief break) I came back from that edge — but not before I stabilized in a depressive, paranoid neurosis in which I often isolated myself from humanity. It was a very slow and gradual integration, but it had its compensations: I had been "there", come back, and managed to integrate the experience into a form meaningful — and not repressive of the psychotic event — to me.

An Analytic Appraisal

In the first part of this paper, I have presented a description of my psychotic experience; I have tried to describe the symptoms of the mental illness from the subjective viewpoint. Now I propose to discuss the psychoanalytic dynamics of the experience: What caused the symptoms? How does this psychotic reaction differ from the neurotic one dynamically? In other words, I try to explain the psychological mechanism which created, drove, and eventually destroyed the psychotic experience.

My psychotic experience actually began with my inability to process the loss of a deeply loved object, my grandfather; in other words, my psychosis was a consequence of an inability to successfully carry through mourning. Such a beginning is characteristic of many psychoses (see e.g. Bowers, 1974); and it is important to understand that psychoses can be the consequence whether separation from the loved object is caused by death, physical separation, or a parting of the ways. To the subconscious, all of these departures are the same.

Of course, inability to successfully carry through mourning can result in either psychosis or severe depressive neurosis. What is the difference between the two? As a consequence of my experience, I can recall gaining personal insight into the dichotomy for I suffered, at separate times, both a psychotic and a neurotic reaction to my grandfather's death. That is, when my grandfather died, I gradually entered a psychotic state which lasted approximately a year; then I suffered a dramatic psychotic break and — with the help of therapy — reentered my neurotic state, a state now quite depressed and paranoid. From this state, a consequence in its severity of my grandfather's death two years previously, I was eventually able to emerge by successfully completing my mourning. In other words, I suffered at separate times both a psychotic reaction to my grandfather's death and a neurotic one. It was at the time of the psychotic break and my entrance into therapy, that I gained some sense of what was happening. I found myself returning to the neurotic state I had known prior to my grandfather's death (but one much more severe), and this return was marked by two interrelated characteristics: the return of a flood of memories, largely repressed in psychosis, of my life at law school, college, and in New York City prior to the psychosis; and the loss of the "sense of light" and the immediacy of memories concerning my grandparents country home which had marked my psychosis.

I felt very ambivalent about this process. In part, I dreaded it: I was gradually losing that peculiar sense of light and beauty which had characterized the psychosis. My sensual world — my sense of taste, touch, sight, hearing, smell —- was becoming an affect-less imitation of its psychotic self; and the emotional concomitant, the joy, which had accompanied this sensual world was receding too. It was as if the sensual world were being covered by a grey scrim. I was being assailed by returning memories of how lonely and unhappy, how depressed and neurotic, I had been during my school years just prior to my psychosis. I felt that I was being carried by an inexorable current back to my familiar neurotic structure. At the same time, I knew that — however painful — the course I was following was absolutely necessary: there was no help for it. If I had permitted myself to penetrate further into the land of psychosis, to interact with "reality" on the basis of an essentially false psychotic identity, I would have found that my return had become even more difficult, if not impossible.

In the beginning of my therapy, I was rewarded by some insights into why these psychological changes had occurred. I sensed that the precipitating event, my grandfather's death, must have acted upon a condition in me already latent; that his death echoed for me some event earlier in my life. One of my first abreactive reactions confirmed this: I was driving from a small Colorado town (where I lived) to the city of Denver to see my psychoanalyst when I suddenly found that I was shaking violently at the wheel of the car, sobbing deeply, and feeling as if once again I were a small child. In that moment, I realized that when as a child (of about two years of age) I had to leave my grandfather and his country home to live with my parents in New York City, I was deeply hurt: I had perceived this as my grandfather's abandonment and betrayal of me. For years, unknown to my consciousness, that sense of hurt and anger against my grandfather had lived on, until the day he died. His death threatened to bring to consciousness these repressed feelings, for it represented a replay of his first departure from me. It was a replay, but it also was a replay with a different ending; subconsciously, a part of me felt a sense of joy: this time in leaving me, he was fittingly punished for the pain he inflicted by separating; he was forced to depart for good ... he died. My inability to acknowledged the joy of a revenge unconsciously nurtured and finally fulfilled, to recognize my ambivalence toward the loved object, marked my precipitation into psychosis.

The trauma I experienced as a young child (and repressed) when I was compelled to separate from my grandfather and my grandmother in their country home also explains many aspects of my character and actions many years later, prior to the psychosis. For example, it became clear to me that my last minute decision not to enter medical school, based at the time on what appeared to be perfectly rational reasons, also was sparked by an element of revenge. I knew how much my grandfather desired someone in his family to follow in his footsteps (neither his son nor daughters had, and none of his other grandchildren evinced an interest), and so I pursued my premedical studies until, at the penultimate moment, I suddenly dropped my interest in a medical career. In effect, what I was saying subconsciously went something like this: "You pretended to be a father to me, then you left me; I will pretend to be like a son to you, and follow in your profession, but at the last minute, I will disappoint you — just like you disappointed me." I did so with a particular vengeance, by embracing a career in which I had shown little interest but the career of my *real* father. In addition, the oscillatory pattern of my personality, during college and law school years, was explainable on the basis of this early separation trauma. During the school term, I studied neurotically and competitively in an urban environment, shunning close friendships; but during the summer, in a country setting, I discarded this role, established close friendships, and let loose the suppressed aspects of my character. This oscillation, as I have indicated, progressively became more violent. The school term represented for me, subconsciously, a period of punishment in which I had to follow the dictates of my father rigidly. Why punishment? Because it was associated with the early separation trauma in which I felt myself banished by my grandfather, handed over to my father, punished for the very aggressive feelings I harbored against my grandfather (this reversal of logic — after all, I felt aggressive *because* I was banished — does not worry the subconscious). I took the school term, under my father's often obsessed guidance, as a prison term I must fulfill in order to be released, for the summer, to a setting which reminded me of my grandparent's home — which in fact when I was younger I had visited during the summers. It was for this reason that so much frenetic, intimate energy was invested during summer vacations from college, and in that year after college; and it was for this reason too that I so brutally terminated those friendships when I returned to school. The terminations represented symbolic acts of revenge for the initial separation trauma I had suffered when the loved object, my grandfather, had left me, a separation trauma which had been repeated in a minor key when at the end of summer vacations at his home I had to depart. So I learned to deny that I was affected by close relationships established during my summers, by quickly and cruelly cutting off these friendship when I returned to school. Lastly, my difficulty in truly rebelling from my father's sway was no doubt influenced by the early effect of the separation trauma; any act of independence was haunted by the act of separation, which had so deeply affected me as a child, from the parental figure of my grandfather.

We are now in a considerably better position to understand what happened to me psychologically when my grandfather died and how my psychotic reaction differed from my neurotic reaction to his death. In both reactions, the key element is the same: the sense of terrible hurt at the loved object departing, and, hard on the heels of this feeling, the sense of terrible anger at the loved object for leaving. This feeling of anger, this "death wish" against the loved object, is the point of origin for both the psychotic and neurotic reaction. One must recognize that it is around this wish that the struggle to accept the finality of death occurs. For the aggressive wish brings with it the problem of "omnipotence of thought": Was the wish itself (even if retroactively, the subconscious makes no allowance for time factors) responsible for the death? How will the mourner deal with the fact that he has not been able to control the loved object — that despite everything he wishes, whether aggressive or resurrective, death has a finality beyond his control? Let us look, first, at my psychotic solution to this problem: In psychosis, on the surface I appeared to have accepted my grandfather's death; I could talk about it; I could cry about it. But, at a more fundamental level, I was unable to accept the finality of that death; to do so would have required recognizing my aggressive feelings toward my grandfather and dealing in some way with my death wish toward him. Instead, I determined, subconsciously, to control the loved object, to prevent its departure, by resurrecting my grandfather in my own personality. To do so, I had to tear myself away from reality on a fundamental level, and construct a new reality, one in which I lived out a drama of being like my grandfather in a setting reminiscent of the country that I associated to him: anything to prevent realization of the permanence of his death.

41

How did my neurotic reaction to my grandfather's death differ? In neurosis, I acknowledged at a fundamental level that my grandfather had died; and as a consequence, at a deep level I recognized also my aggressive feelings toward him. But now, still wishing to hold off the full point of my lack of control over the loved object, I sought another tactic: "Yes," I said to myself at some interior level of my personality, "he is dead, and I did have aggressive feelings toward him. In fact, it must have been my aggressive feelings that were responsible for the death." With that, I experienced the sense of neurotic guilt and paranoid depression which characterized my personality after the psychotic break. As severe as this state was, however, it had some decided virtues; unlike the psychosis, in which reality is denied on a much more fundamental level and a false identity is erected to defend against this reality, the neurosis was considerably more amenable to psychotherapy.

The distinction I am making here has been made before with slightly different emphasis and more structure. Freud in two classic short papers dealt with the dichotomy between neurosis and psychosis. In his first paper, Neurosis and Psychosis (1924a), he stated that: "(N)eurosis is the result of a conflict between the ego and its id, whereas psychosis is the analogous outcome of a similar disturbance in the relations between the ego and the external world." That is, in neurosis, the ego refuses to "accept a powerful instinctual impulse in the id," and denies the impulse motor discharge. Then, at the dictates of the superego, the ego calls up the mechanism of repression. But the "repressed material struggles against this fate. It creates for itself, along paths over which the ego has no power, a substitutive representation . . . " In contrast, in psychosis, the id impulses triumph by collapsing the ego's relation with the outer world . As Freud observes there is a "close affinity of this psychosis with normal dreams", except that dreams occur in sleep.

In his second paper, "The Loss of Reality in Neurosis and Psychosis" (1924b), Freud elaborated further on this distinction by giving the following case study of a neurosis:

> (A) young woman was in love with her brother-in-law. Standing beside her sister's death-bed, she was horrified at the thought: "Now he is free and can marry me." This scene was instantly forgotten, and thus the process of repression which led to her hysterical pains was set in motion. It is instructive precisely in this case, moreover, to learn along what path the neurosis attempted to solve the conflict. It took away from the value of the change that had occurred in reality, by repressing the instinctual demand which had emerged — that is, her love for her brother-in-law. The psychotic reaction would have been a disavowal of the fact of the sister's death. (p.183)

And he expands on the differences between the two defenses, neurosis and psychosis, to the expression of the id impulses:

> (T)he initial difference is expressed . . . in the final outcome: in neurosis a part of reality is avoided by a sort of flight, but in psychosis it is remodelled. Or we might say: in psychosis, the initial flight is succeeded by an active phase of remodelling; in neurosis, the initial obedience is succeeded by a deferred attempt at flight. Or again, expressed in another way, neurosis does not disavow the reality, it only ignores it; psychosis disavows it and tries to replace it. (p. 184)

Let us now examine a little more closely exactly what it was my psychosis, in reaction to my repressed death wish against my grandfather and joy of revenge at his death, tried to substitute for reality. To begin with, I sought out an environment which I strongly identified with my grandfather: the country and a small town setting rather than the busy city (which my grandfather had always detested). In doing so, I sought to avoid the superficialities of big city living, which I associated with my father, and return to the verities (as I conceived them) inherent in a small town — making as I did so the same choice as my grandfather had as a young doctor. I also identified other actions of mine with my grandfather or his country home: the beauties of the countryside were associated in my mind with the Adirondacks where I had been raised as an infant or as a child during summers; music from a phonograph was strongly associated to that county home, for my father never played the phonograph but my grandfather listened regularly to classical music; my setting off from home was strongly associated with my grandfather's solitary journey as a young man from his native Russia, leaving his family behind, to a foreign land; my sense of certainty in evaluating people came in part from my identification with my grandfather — who made quick and to my young eyes seemingly certain judgments about people. In other words, although I recognized that I was a separate individual, I strongly identified (replacing some of my own characteristics in the process) with the deceased loved object. I was resurrecting him in me.

This attempt succeeded surprising well during the functional stage: I worked competently, I dealt with people in the straight-forward manner I conceived my grandfather doing, and I felt a joy of triumph in escaping the bondage of my life in New York City. In fact, my memories of New York, of my neurotic years, tended to recede in favor of memories of my grandfather's country town. The job I held also had the virtue, from the point of view of the psychosis, of being isolated from and opposed to the "civilized" world from which I was attempting to keep my distance. In my representation of the Navajos, I was representing intrapsychically the desires of my id, which wished to challenge the social conventions and introjected superego associated with my culture.

Things went well as long as I maintained a psychological distance from others, but as might be expected the acting out was not to remain long on such an even keel. When I began to become intimate with Darlene, whose child I strongly identified with, I was beginning to act out the logical conclusion of the psychosis. Darlene who had come from such a poorly educated (in Western culture terms) family and who with such spirit had struggled against terrible odds to better herself, represented for me my own maternal grandmother. And her child with whom I so strongly identified tended to represent myself at the age I lived in my grandparent's home. In other words, the logical culmination of my id's wishes was not only to kill off my grandfather but to marry my grandmother; first it killed off (or thought it did) my grandfather, then resurrected him in me — he never truly died, and then it played out the fantasy further by having me marry my grandmother in substitutive form.

My developing struggle with figures of authority, the head of the legal services organization and my friend who reminded me of my grandfather, should be seen as an interrelated part of my wish to culminate the fantasy with the grandmother substitute. For the closer I came to fulfilling this fantasy, the more my aggressive wishes toward my grandfather were likely to come to the surface. It was as if the statement, "I am really glad he died, because now I can have grandmother all to myself," was threatening to bubble into consciousness. To guard against this, what developed was a feeling of paranoia vis-à-vis authority figures who reminded me of my grandfather: I was now dealing with my developing realization of my aggression by projecting it onto grandfather figures. Another aspect of this paranoia should also be apparent, and that is that it related to my homosexual wishes toward my grandfather: I wished also to be his woman, to substitute for my grandmother. (Again, the subconscious does not deal with the concept of mutual exclusivity: it has no reality principle to inform it that two things cannot be in the same place at the same time.) Freud has traced, in his classic study of Schreber's paranoia, the relationship of homosexuality to paranoid manifestations (Freud, 1911). The projection of aggressive intent upon grandfather-figures represented an attempt to deny the sexual attraction and desire for submission on my part. It is no accident, then, that at the psychotic break stage this desire came to the fore, and I was tempted to, but did not, act upon a homosexual impulse in a situation with a relative stranger.

It was thus inevitable that as I approached the possibility of marriage with the grandmother-figure, my psychotic structure would be threatened to the breaking point. The hesitation and indecision, the inability to stay still, which characterized this disintegration stage, were symptoms of the psychosis tottering on the brink of annihilation. Finally, events shattered the psychotic "dream" and when the connections with a fantasied reality disintegrated, so did the psychosis. Dependent as it was for its sustenance upon the Navajo reservation, upon the wish for culmination with a grandmother figure, it could not survive on the nourishment reality offered in other places. My personality began to break up — and in this self-administered disintegration, I also (as a parting and particularly brutal blow evident of the aggression hidden behind the mystical exterior of the psychosis) administered a punishment against the figure which reminded me of myself at the age when my grandfather separated from me: I left Darlene's child. In other words, I played the role my grandfather had played with me as a child, in inducing my sense of separation trauma. Perhaps nothing in my actions was more a witness to the desire for revenge, and the wish for self-punishment as a consequence of this aggressive intent (all of which resulted from this early separation trauma) than this.

The disintegration was a product of an ego which no longer had a model: having failed in the psychotic attempt, I no longer knew who I was, what memories were significant, how to act. Gradually I returned to my neurotic self, felt the memories associated with the psychosis lose their vibrancy, and the memories of New York City return. As might be expected, I also introjected into my character that of Darlene whom I had left. I was now undertaking a double mourning, for the death of my grandfather and for the separation from the Navajo woman Darlene. Needless to say, my therapy dealt with not only my anger and hurt at my grandfather "leaving" me at a young age, but of my grandmother leaving me as well, the figure whom Darlene represented.

But what of the peculiar "heightened state of reality" which accompanied my psychosis and the psychotic choice in general? How does it fit into the dynamics? In denying the finality of the separation from the loved object, I sought to regress to that period of time before the initial separation trauma by introjecting (not obviously in my case) my grandfather in myself. At all costs, I was going to deny the finality of that death, and in my introjection I created a world in which separation was impossible, a kind of "before being banned from the garden" experience. That sense of oneness and identity with the object word *in general* was part and parcel of my refusal to recognize separation from a loved object in particular. But at the same time, I made a calculated gamble: I attempted to gain a kind of psychic renewal of interest and enjoyment in the world, a breath of fresh air — away from the stale hopelessness which accompanied my neurotic depression — to remind me of the possibilities of the world. I was very fortunate, when the psychotic break came, to survive the gamble by recourse to effective psychoanalysis. Without therapy, I would not have been able to create a synthesis in which the neurotic veil was lifted enough to permit a more integrated version of the "visionary gleam" — without resort to the far country.

III. Reflections in the Present — 50 years Later

I t is interesting for me to look back at the events fifty years ago and the article written forty years ago. Although I had no formal analytic training at that time — only self-education through reading in psychoanalysis during the course of my analysis and afterward — I am struck that I would subscribe today to the same phenomenology and dynamics I discussed back then in explaining the psychotic and neurotic aspects of my experience. Today, I might alter the style in which I wrote of these experiences, which seems at times melodramatic, but I remind myself that today I am established and more or less emotionally secure; back then, my survival depended on my only recently completed first analysis, I was psychologically still somewhat precarious, and my future remained uncertain.

The Process of Analysis

However, one thing missing from the article is the process of that first analysis, which permitted me to function again, as well as the effect of a second and more complete analysis. Re-

reading the article, I realize that much of my formal analytic thinking and subsequent clinical work with patients has been guided in part by the experiences I just described and the two analyses which addressed them. I am particularly impressed by the malleability of character, the extent to which it derives from early object relations and attachments, and how it is shaped by these identifications — a point which I elaborate upon below with reference to the identificatory role the psychoanalyst plays for the patient in treatment.

I had no real awareness of psychoanalytic thought until I lay down on the couch back then. Although psychologically shaky, I took to psychoanalysis immediately : it was clear to me that it addressed an emptiness in my understanding of the world, a gap in my knowledge, of which I had been dimly aware. As an English major, I had often analyzed character in novels and poetry, and as one who minored in creative writing, I had also created characters in fledgling short stories, short plays, and a novella, but Freudian thought opened up a whole new psychodynamic country for me, as if a scrim had been pulled away on a new (but at the same time familiar) landscape. I felt I had come home. I devoured Freud's writings, beginning with the Interpretation of Dreams. I also devoured the writings of my own analyst, an unusually talented and prolific psychoanalytic writer and thinker in his own right, and I went through almost all the psychoanalytic references cited in his most prominent book.

Here there was both a solution and another problem. I very much identified with this analyst. He became a new object, the father I had not had, the grandfather for whom I would have wished, and the mother with a creative bent who was reliable as opposed to problematic. Loewald (1960) says it best in his paper "On the therapeutic action of psychoanalysis":

> *Analysis is . . . understood as an intervention designed to set ego-development in motion, be it from a point of relative arrest, or to promote what we conceive of as a healthier direction and /or comprehensiveness of such development. This is achieved by the promotion and utilization of (controlled) regression. This regression is one important aspect under which the transference neurosis can be understood. The transference neurosis, in the sense of reactivation of the childhood neurosis, is set in motion not simply by the technical skill of the analyst, but by the fact that the analyst makes himself available for the development of a new "object-relationship" between the patient and the analyst. (p. 17)*

Or as he says later on:

> *This new discovery of oneself and of objects, this reorganization of ego and objects, is made possible by the encounter with a "new object" which has to possess certain*

qualifications in order to promote the process. Such a new object-relationship for which the analyst holds himself available to the patient and to which the patient has to hold on throughout the analysis is one meaning of the term "positive transference". (p. 18)

I thrived in this new object-relationship and it felt as if a growth process had begun again, albeit in the midst of a depression. In many ways, I was "driving on fumes" however. That is, my intellect carried me forward so that I could function — and sometimes surprisingly well from outside appearances — but emotionally I was often unattached, flat, desperate, obsessive inside, and alone. The analysis provided a cognitive framework, which was so important to giving me a sense of my identity, and a narrative to explain my experiences. The analysis tended toward being too cerebral, however, and sometimes there was an emotionally ungiving, even competitive quality in the analyst's interaction with me. (Years later, when the analyst had become more of a colleague, unsolicited he told me that he wished he had not been so "hard" on me.) Ultimately I was rescued in the midst of this by a loving woman, whose humor, warmth and attentiveness brought me back (although unfortunately for both of us years later the relationship did not thrive, but that is another story) and whom I married. But in terms of identity, at that time I found myself adopting ways of processing and thinking which I associated with my analyst. In this way, the psychotic process and the deep depression were stopped. After the analysis, I ended up writing psychoanalytic articles in a style somewhat similar to his. Because of the analysis, I determined to fashion a career as an analyst, obtained a master's degree in psychology, moved back East to New York City to pursue my doctoral degree in psychology, and then upon obtaining it, trained as a psychoanalyst. In my second and much longer analysis with a very patient and determined analyst, I was able to work through the overidentification with the first analyst (the transference cure which had been so helpful to me) as well as unresolved aspects of my relationship to my parents, particularly my mother.

Here I must add that, although I describe my mother's character at the beginning of the article, and mention that her lack of constancy as a maternal figure heightened the emotional importance of other parental figures (my grandmother, my grandfather, my father) in my life, I fail to state explicitly that this rendered me particularly emotionally susceptible to the loss of those figures. Nor in terms of object relations and identification, do I mention a salient fact: my mother had a certain underlying paranoid cast to her defenses, which became apparent when she was anxious, and which contributed to my own sense of paranoia. (I have alluded to this in a recent piece I have written on paranoia in terms of my countertransference reactions to a paranoid patient.) . Thus, the ability of my second analyst, incidentally a woman, to pursue the focus on my mother in the transference was crucial. This was aided by the fact that my second analyst was much less inclined to make pronouncements as interventions than my previous analyst had been (he was more "old school" if you will [trained at New York Psychoanalytic in its heyday]) and as a result there was more space for the maternal aspect of the transference to develop in the second analysis.

The Black Maid and Sexual Dynamics

In my 1978 article, I self-protectively left out another crucial early loss and some related sexual material that figured in the psychotic development. Let me explain by trying to reproduce how this other early loss became apparent to me. The loss attached to an action I took that embarrassed me so greatly that I could not admit to it in the article — when Navajo woman Darlene announced she was leaving me for another, I became so distraught that I actually slapped her in front of her four year old daughter, who of course cried out. That I had slapped her and that I had frightened her young daughter, undoubtedly traumatizing her, left me as inconsolable as did losing her love. This terrible moment, for which I felt overwhelming remorse for many, many years, seemed electric at the time and in slow-motion. In that moment, I seemed to relive an event from my past — there was a deja vu feeling about it. I did not know exactly what I was reliving but I knew I was reliving something that had happened to me as a child. What it was became clear to me — my memory of it more fully revived (the memory was never entirely gone, but it acquired increased lucidity, valence and meaning) — in the course of my first analysis.

Still telling background: When my parents moved to Manhattan, they eventually moved to a spacious top, eighth floor apartment overlooking Central Park. I was four years old. Out of my bedroom window, I could see the great green park stretched out, and it reminded me of the Adirondack countryside and my grandparents that I had had to leave. During the day, I would sometimes be in the playground of the park which at other times I could actually see from my bedroom window.

On some days back then, my mother left our apartment to practice law with my father in midtown Manhattan, and I was entrusted to the care of a Black maid who also did the cleaning. As I recall, over time there was more than one Black maid. A young one, whom I was very fond of, permitted me to lie down with her and let me caress her back and breast, and approach near her vagina. The young one disappeared. But as importantly, I also remember, another of these maids, an older and more matronly woman, of whom I became particularly fond, especially because she prepared my breakfast as soon as my mother left. Unlike my grandmother, my mother was not a good cook, and did not like cooking; and so this matronly Black woman reminded me very much of the grandmother in Elizabethtown whom I felt had left me. I still have a vision of her in the kitchen wearing an apron and serving me scrambled eggs.

One day, and I believe it happened more than once, she arrived with a young Black boy, somewhat older than me, either a son or grandson. We were left to play together in a room, while she did the cleaning in other rooms. I remember admiring this Black boy. I cannot recall the details exactly but he exposed his penis to me and had me touch it, at which point the Black maid entered the room. For years I believed she slapped me when she saw what was going on, but now I think it much more likely that she slapped him. I did cry out however. I remember that feeling of amazement that he, whom I admired so much, was not invulnerable. The Black maid apparently left at the end of that day without explanation, never to return, and I never recounted what had happened to my mother. This was the slap that I seemed to relive when I slapped my Navajo girlfriend, and the crying four year old child felt as if it was me at four years old crying with the slap as well. The slap was the crucial recovered part of the memory during the analysis.

The traumatic effect on me of this childhood event was very great. Immediately, as a child, I acted out, which I explain below. And years subsequently I also acted out in ways (which I also explain below) that provide additional meaning to my working down South for SCLC as a civil rights worker and going to the Navajo reservation to become a legal services attorney.

Immediately (and this memory required no reviving, as it has always been vivid, although the psychodynamic reason for it was reconstructed in the analysis): On one of the subsequent days, with my mother now at home, and my being confined to my bedroom where I was supposed to take a nap, while she was in the living room, I decided that I would obey her rule about not opening my bedroom door, by going out the window instead and climbing around the building and surprise her by entering the window in the living room. So I opened my bedroom window, climbed over the metal guard rail, so I was now standing on the window ledge itself, and put one foot on the smaller ledge that went between windows and around the building. The next window did not belong to our apartment and I envisioned looking into it, as I supposedly made my way around the entire building. But even though I was only four years old, I knew that shifting my weight onto the foot I had placed on the smaller ledge was problematic. So I literally froze up there on the eight floor, contemplating making that move. I did not want to turn back and give up but

I was afraid to go on as it was too dangerous. Meanwhile, on the park pavement down below, some man repeatedly yelled up at me, which annoyed me because it interfered with my concentration, and I noticed that other people down there had stopped and were craning their necks to look up at me as well. This man, actually a college student, took it upon himself to rush into the building, take the elevator to the eighth floor, bang on the door to the apartment, rush into the apartment as soon as my mother answered the door — asking her where her child was, run down the hallway to my room and fling the door to my bedroom open with my astonished mother in pursuit behind him (shocked when she did not see me in the room and the window wide open). He then went to the open window, reached over the guard rail and pulled me in. That evening, my father spanked me and nailed all the windows in the apartment so they could not open too far. My parents subsequently switched apartments with a couple we knew (he was a well-known Ash Can school painter), so that we now lived in a much smaller second floor artist's studio with a giant skylight. (Supposedly, a fall from a second floor apartment window was less likely to be fatal.)

To tie this together: The natural world outside my window, the great green expanse of Central Park embedded in the city streets, represented to me Elizabethtown and my grandmother, whom I had been forced to leave. So when the Black maid, a grandmotherly substitute, disappeared too, and left me too (and because of something I had done) I decided I could not be confined any further— I would make an escape into the air, be in the open of green Central Park, and climb around the building, not incidentally looking in a next door window — perhaps I too would see something forbidden. (I would not discount the possibility as well that this was the desire to witness a primal scene type of interaction, as I might have seen with my parents, but I have no memory to confirm this hypothesis.) My first analyst thought my actions represented a four-year-old's suicidal gesture, which perhaps they did. But (and here is the final object relational point)— I was devastated by the loss of the Black maid, as I had been devastated by the loss of my grandmother in Elizabethtown whom she represented.[2]

And now one can see a further determinant for my working down South and for my going to the Navajo reservation and having a Navajo girlfriend. Unbeknownst to my consciousness, I was searching not only for my grandmother but for the Black maid who had left me. However, when I actually found someone who substituted for her I was unable to take the relationship to its natural conclusion. (I might add here — for further evidence — that I also had love relationships around the same time that I went to the Navajo reservation, with two Black women, both dynamic civil rights attorneys, whom I left as I left the Navajo woman, in the same self-destructive need to get revenge because of my early object loss — to leave them before they would leave me as she had.) When I slapped the Navajo woman who left me, I slapped symbolically the Black maid from my childhood, slapping her for the abandonment, just as she had seemed to slap me. To add one further piquant note, which shows how multi-determined things can be, when I said in the 1978 article that Darlene left me for another, I neglected to add (also because of shame or embarrassment) that the other man was a medical doctor just like my grandfather, albeit a hippy one, and thus the Oedipal loss and dynamics with regard to my grandmother were even further implicated. (Because of the significance of the Black maid and my symbolic search for her, when I first read Interpretation of Dreams and Freud's letters, I felt a deep affinity with Freud due to his childhood experience of his old Christian nanny, whose sudden departure left him traumatized and in mourning, and not just as a substitute for his mother, but in her own right as an attachment figure. As we know, this brought Freud to his first screen memory, the search for his seemingly lost mother boxed up in a cupboard [Freud, . One of the consequences of my fascination with this subject, was that early on I communicated with Hardin who published the first of a series of articles on the significance of the nanny in children's development [Hardin, 1985]. I wrote to him years before any formal psychoanalytic training on my part. And ultimately, all of this led me to publish my own psychoanalytic article on the nature of screen memory involving material from one of my control cases [Reichbart, 2008].)

In terms of the psychosis I embraced by traveling to the reservation, I apparently sought to enact a scenario that did not encompass the loses I had experienced in childhood or acknowledge the aggression that I felt as a result of them. I created a drama that denied the object loss embodied in the Black maid, and before that in my grandmother and grandfather. Ultimately, in order to come to terms with these, I had to return to the neurotic aspect of my personality and a now even greater depression. I needed to experience that depression fully in order to seek help and get well.

Let me now characterize that "greater depression" further than I have so far and more specifically. The feeling was one of continual psychological pressure, and physical pressure on my head, like a low intensity but continual tension headache; and the paranoid sense I experienced during that extended time were that others might know how I had treated Darlene, my Navajo girlfriend at the end, for which I felt so guilty. The reservation was hundreds of miles away in a different state, and I was living in an urban center, so the thoughts were not realistic (which I also at the same time knew) but they were pervasive. I did represent members of other Native American tribes as an attorney and there was an outside possibility that these Native Americans might have known what happened on the reservation but this was only briefly. Subsequently I literally "dropped out" of being a lawyer entirely (I drove a taxi-cab on night shift, and then opened an art gallery with my wife) with the paranoid feelings continuing although they gradually were alleviated. I also was familiar with the witchcraft beliefs that permeate traditional Navajo culture and sometimes felt that Darlene's grandmother (whom I had never actually met, but often the matriarchs in Navajo society are thought to have psychic powers) knew of how I had treated her granddaughter and magically condemned me.

As happens in cases of neurotic paranoid depression for part of this time I tended to isolate myself, and I spent a lot of time compulsively reading in psychoanalysis, psychology and culture (eventually actually publishing journal articles in aspects of these fields). In effect, I survived using my intellect, but the internal experience was one of neurotic depression with some paranoid features.

The Acid Experience

One final note, for those who may have noticed the shaking experience that occurred when I retrieved the traumatic memory of having to leave my grandparents as a small child (a shaking incidentally accompanied by a warm feeling throughout my body and some difficulty drawing a breath) and also for those who might wonder about pre-Oedipal trauma. I mentioned that my mother frequently had her head in a book, leaving me very much on my own, even when I was very young. The consequence of this was that I had a series of other nearly fatal catastrophes as a child. At the age of 3, I apparently got into the car parked in my grandparents' driveway, and managed to set the seat on fire with a spark from the cigarette lighter (with me in the car) and had to be rescued. Again, my mother complained in my adult years that when I was a little older than 3, when we briefly lived in suburban New Jersey, I liked to wander into the street in front of our house and nearly got hit by cars (in recounting this she had no awareness whatsoever of her lack of attentiveness).

But most traumatic was an event that took place in the Elizabethtown house when I was only 1 ½ years old. Left unattended in this extremely large house, I apparently made my way by crawling or toddling into my grandmother's dental office which was in a room in the back of the house. My grandmother was not there. Alone in the office, I managed to raise myself up enough to reach a bottle on a shelf or table top. The bottle was filled with acid used for dental work, and in reaching it, I knocked it down so the acid poured down one arm and on to my chest.

Fortunately, my doctor grandfather was home and his quick action by washing me down probably saved my life, which made me over subsequent years feel particularly close to him. My chest ended up with raised welts and one arm and elbow had a long welt where the acid had poured down, all of which gradually lost their red coloration over the years although they remained visible. And clearly I was fortunate that no acid hit my face or eyes. But emotionally, the act of reaching for a bottle with its oral association, reaching for something in the room I knew as my grandmother's, may have helped to create the feeling that attempting to achieve a connection to a maternal object, could result in sudden and terrible pain. Speculatively, this may have contributed to the creation of a psychotic tendency — a fear of connecting fully with the object.

Another and more certain consequence of this event I also should mention. The consequence related to my decision not to attend medical school many years later, although I did not understand any of this until my first analysis. At Yale College, I all but failed an important course that was necessary to attend a top-notch medical school (and in my thinking at the time if I did not go to a top-notch school, my father would be disappointed, and so this contributed to my feeling that I should not pursue a career in medicine). The deficient grade was in organic chemistry lab, although I did well in the theoretical organic chemistry course that accompanied it. In fact, I felt so anxious in the laboratory itself that I could not concentrate, could not be organized, and constantly made mistakes. I used to have to walk out of the lab to be in the fresh air briefly to collect myself before returning to try again; and I would find myself to my surprise literally shaking internally, which I took to be nerves. Even working in the lab after class hours to catch up did not seem to help significantly. My skills were so abysmal that at one point I exploded a flask I was heating, singeing my face and hair, which required me to stay in the college infirmary for a day. What I did not realize until my analysis, was that the acid experience as a toddler had so traumatized me that its effect on my body was still with me , as was a shaking reaction. Twenty years after I reached for the bottle of acid as a toddler, knocking it over, and the acid poured onto my flesh, searing it, I became internally terrified once again when I reached for glass bottles and flasks of acid, or turned on the flame of a Bunsen burner. Oedipally, one might also equate this with the thought that to my mind my grandfather could handle acid, having become a doctor, and could be with my grandmother, from whom the acid came, and I felt this role was forbidden to me. (If it is at all evidentiary, I should add that I re-took organic chemistry lab at a local university during my first analysis and after this discovery — my hope being that I might reapply to medical school with this grade improved. This time, I experienced no difficulty in the laboratory, actually loved the course, and did well in it.)

Another Fear of An Object Loss

Briefly let me add that the experience of shaking in the car, accompanied by the retrieval of a childhood memory related to object loss, happened one other time, and on the same automobile drive to my first analyst's office. In this instance, I suddenly recalled that when I was very young my father expressed his anger at me by refusing to speak to me for days. I had not thought of this for a long time. Now I began to shake internally and then sob openly in the car (I was amazed actually both these times that I was able to hold onto the wheel sufficiently to continue driving) for I realized how cruel my father's silence had been. It had frightened me terribly: It made me believe that my father too would leave me just as my grandfather and grandmother had, and as a punishment. Until that moment, I had no memory of the emotional meaning of his many days' silence, even if I remembered the silence. I had to wait for more than two decades when at the beginning of my analysis the suppressed trauma announced itself in this electric-like bodily re-emergence. .

My "Case" Today

Lastly, one might ask how might my psychoanalytic "case" be handled today. Back then, my first analyst believed implicitly in the transformational power of intense psychoanalysis and did everything that was possible — seeing me seven days a week at the beginning, refusing to put me on an anti-psychotic or anti-anxiety drug (he wanted to get me off medication as soon as possible), not wanting to hospitalize me unless absolutely necessary because he thought of it as counterproductive — to turn my treatment into a continuing five day weekly analysis sans medication . From the beginning, he invited me to think of what had happened psychodynamically, rather than to think of myself as subject to familial depression or some type of organic disorder, and thereby he immediately enlisted my curiosity. He plunged right in. In addition, his apparent lack of anxiety despite the seriousness of my symptoms, his fearlessness if you will, was tremendously important to me. And all in all his approach worked wonderfully. It not only relieved my symptoms but it profoundly changed my life. However, such a determined approach does pose the question whether most contemporary analysts — when frequency of sessions generally has been reduced and anti-psychotic, anti-anxiety medications are more readily employed — would explore my defensive structure and my psychodynamics with such frequency and intensity from the very first day of treatment.

I think that my experience has permitted me to be less fazed by seemingly psychotic manifestations in a patient than I might otherwise be and endlessly curious about how that patient thinks and feels. However, I do not think of what I experienced as anything approaching schizophrenia or schizotypal disorder, which I have seen particularly when working in an inpatient setting (with the caveat that I do wonder what would have happened without successful intervention). Regardless, it would be in my judgment a mistake to confuse this type of psychotic episode with anything approaching schizophrenia. What has always struck me is the unrelenting, psychodynamic logic of my thoughts and feelings, even when I was struggling, and my ability to articulate that logic in speaking with another. Often, however, in the psychoanalytic literature, the differences between this type of psychotic experience and more severe disorders are obviated.

Finally, some might think that what I recount is not in the nature of psychosis, and yet I do not know any other word (other than possibly a long disassociative experience) that fits — particularly in its shaking beginning and its devastating depressive denouement, in the feeling of bright light that permeated it over an extended period of time, in the forcing of an interior drama onto reality, and in the way objects in that reality became symbolic of the interior drama. Although one might see not only anxiety but some manic manifestations at the end of the psychotic experience (as if I were frantically searching for some magical way to stave off the return to neurotic depression), there was no sense in the heart of the experience itself of anything manic. Nonetheless, more than one colleague has suggested that what I label "psychotic experience" was more in the nature of a manic episode, as part of a manic-depressive syndrome, and one of these colleagues was curious to know if there had ever been a recurrence of depression beyond that recounted here. There has not been, although in and of itself that probably should not be determinative of whether manic-depression applies. But I do not know that "mania" does justice to how I felt for an extended period of time, perhaps because the word conjures up a less organized and more organic pathology (although I may have a too-constricted view of the meaning of the word). For me, the internal logic of the changes I experienced seems paramount as does the feeling of being "lived" by that logic as a driving force, and I find myself leery of a diagnostic label that ends up minimizing that logic.

As an analyst, I have experienced that when certain analytic patients manage, after many years of treatment, to finally dispel the depression that permeated their feelings and lives, it is as if a grey scrim between them and the world has been lifted. These patients marvel at seeing the world brightly again, at feeling their bodies alive again, and at experiencing happiness and a connection with the world they had all but forgotten existed. Initially when this happens, such patients sometimes all but hold their breath, afraid they will fall back into or be pulled back into their depression. But in these cases, the patients find that the new world they seem to be encountering, and their new feelings, are permanent; the feelings come about because the person has successfully overcome a repression and its sequaelae, modified a punitive superego, and integrated his aggression. One might remark that when the depression lifts, different memories do surface or have greater valence than they did before, and characterological change does seem to have taken place. But their new state is not structurally fragile, as my new psychotic state was. Their new state derives through psychoanalysis from integrating formerly repressed feelings rather than denying them or splitting them off; and their ability now to negotiate the world is improved . These patients do not use the stuff of the world to create a symbolic, personal drama, to try to sustain the new state.

Conclusion

In our work, we necessarily have to generalize about psychosis, dynamics, mourning, and psychoanalytic transformations in treatment. Each analysis, each patient, as we know only too well is unique. I do hope however that this recounting, particularly with its emphasis on the object relations and identifications that contributed to a psychotic experience, break, and depression, will prove helpful to our understanding of such events.

****

IV. An Interesting Addendum

I am not sure why I left out this recognition from both accounts of these events. Perhaps I did not fully comprehend it or it seemed far-fetched. It seems less so now. Perhaps recent literature, psychoanalytic and otherwise. which has focused on Whiteness and Blackness prompted me to locate this sequel to my acid experience which I had not permitted myself to fully explore previously. Or perhaps the impact on a woman psychoanalytic patient who for years as a child was compelled to wear a metal brace to correct her scoliosis and the effect of that on her development (where she managed unfortunately to persuade her parents not to touch her) impressed me. But the fact is that the acid that fell on my chest (and also on the back of my right forearm and elbow) left a very discernible mark, much more so when I was a child and less so as time has gone on: a chest-wide reddish splash of a welt, obvious and remarkable, which as I got older gradually turned more flesh colored, whiter than the rest of my chest as scar tissue will, and became considerably less striking over time, so that today it is hardly noticeable.

I now realize that as an infant and as a child when my chest was exposed, people stared at that wide red splotch; it would have been hard not to do so. At the beach, for example, people looked at my chest. I think I got used to this and simply accepted it so that it left my consciousness, as if to say it made little apparent difference to me and perhaps unconsciously as a reaction formation I wore it as a silent, mysterious badge of which I was proud. However, I believe it made me particularly attuned to skin color, sympathetic toward people with different skin than my white skin, and aware if just beneath my consciousness of people staring at me as an anomaly. Of course, in the way a child thinks of things, I felt I was a "redskin" on my chest (the pejorative associations of this term would not have occurred to me as a child in the 1940's) and perhaps all of this in some way unconsciously contributed to my choosing to work with Native Americans and my feelings when I was doing so.

****

V. The Reaction of Psychoanalysts to This Discussion of Psychosis

There have been various reactions by psychoanalysts and therapists to this presentation and to my wish to publish it. I thought it useful to share them. Originally, this paper, more or less as it appears now, was presented on April 20, 2012 at the Division 39 (Psychoanalysts and Psychoanalytic Psychotherapists) of the American Psychological Association summer conference entitled "The Leading Edge of Creativity" in Santa Fe, New Mexico — a more than appropriate place to present it given that my experience took place on the Navajo reservation not very far from Santa Fe —with psychoanalyst Robert Liss, J.D., Ph.D, a high school friend and fellow graduate of Yale Law School, as moderator and Nancy McWilliams, PhD as discussant. (Reichbart, 2012) Both have been stalwart in supporting me and I am particularly grateful to Dr. McWilliams for her unstinting encouragement then and now.

A number of psychoanalysts disagreed with aspects of this presentation and sometimes offered impassioned advice about presenting it. The first objection that I heard, from the distinguished analyst Shelly Bach, PhD recently deceased, whose work I have greatly admired, was clear and heartfelt: "Don't publish it," he advised. He felt it would reflect badly on me. In fact, I held Shelly in such high esteem and with such strong feelings of closeness not just because of his work but because he reminded me of my grandfather that his negative reaction to publishing (like an adjuration from my grandfather) discouraged me for a long time from doing so.

A related objection occurred when I presented an abbreviated version of it at a meeting of the New Jersey Psychoanalytic Society the Hackensack Medical Center in 2011: more than one psychoanalyst pleaded with me not to label the experience a "psychotic" one. Their argument seemed to be that it was bi-polar experience instead, and they implied for reasons beyond me that bi-polar was a less serious diagnosis than a psychotic break, something with which I do not necessarily agree. Regardless, I do not think bi-polar fluctuations, with their sometimes impenetrable cognitive walls between different emotional states, reflects my experience. In addition, of course, as fine a diagnostician as Nancy McWilliams, whose work on diagnosis is much more formidable than mine and is widely accepted believed this to be a psychotic experience (and apparently despite the fact that the Diagnostic Statistical Manual V appears to now insist that psychosis must involve hallucinations without insight into their pathology or delusions

[delusions being somewhat undefined]) (American Psychiatric Association, 2013).

In contrast to those who asked me to be wary of publishing this experience, there were those — in addition to Dr. McWilliams — who felt it was important to publish it. For example, a colleague of mine, Michael Moskowitz (who has himself bravely created a brief video vignette[2] of an analytic session of him with his own psychoanalyst, Dr. Kirkland Vaughans) felt strongly that I should publish it (although he too thought it was not a psychotic experience). Dr. Moskowitz believes that psychoanalysts too readily deny or disguise their own therapeutic and emotional experiences. He contends, as do I, that this reluctance denies psychoanalysts our common humanity, distancing us from our patients and our colleagues, and deprives us of psychoanalytic insights.

There is a part of this, however , which I have not succeeded in communicating fully in what I presented so far, which pertains to this disagreement about diagnosis. One of the most cogent emotional aspect of this experience was my feeling close to certainty that without the psychoanalytic intervention I received, I would have continued further into psychosis. There was nothing bi-polar about such a feared descent; it was all of a piece, tending toward a feeling of impending " personality loss".

Contributing to this feeling of impending "personality loss" were two accompanying and related phenomena.

The first of which I have already spoken was the continual headache pressure that took place for many years but gradually dissipated, mingled with the paranoid-like sense that I had betrayed both the Navajo woman Darlene and her child and would be found out, particularly in some magical way by Darlene's grandmother whom I conceived to have the properties of a witch (the psychic powers of witches are integral to Navajo culture and I have written about them in other contexts [Reichbart, 2019, pp .163-200]). Self-punishment yes, and interesting because it suggests a fear of my own grandmother, but it was continual and without any bi-polar fluctuations at all for a long time.

The second phenomenon also took many years to dissipate. It took place in some dreams that occurred at times and had a common thread. Here is a description of one particularly vivid one from roughly ten years ago.

I willed myself awake last night with much effort. I had experienced a nightmare, not of a violent or gruesome kind but of a kind that in various guises, I have experienced before and from which at those times I had also in those dreams desperately willed myself awake. In fact, this was a characteristic of these dreams — they ended with a compelling need to somehow awaken, the terrible feeling of an underwater swimmer trying repeatedly without success to reach the surface — until finally

I burst forth into the safety of the familiar: a bed, walls, a sleeping companion, a time, a place I recognized.

In this instance, the day before I had in my anxiety been very cruel to a loved one which I deeply regretted, and I knew as soon as I awoke that this was the reason for my dream. That terrible need to awaken arose from the feeling in the dream that I no longer knew where I was. How could I get back to reality if I could not envision it? How could I awaken from being asleep if I did not know where I was sleeping? In this instance, at the end of an elaborate series of dream events I had been left with a handful of keys; apparently the keys fit doors from my past to which I could no longer return. Most frighteningly, however, was the sense that not only did I not know where I was in reality, I did not know who I was. I no longer knew my personality. I did not want to end up as the seemingly superficial personality I felt I had become in the dream, a personality without strong convictions.

This was in the nature of a punishment dream in which I made myself pay a price for the cruelty I felt I had committed on the previous day, just as I punished myself with the continual headache for my treatment of Darlene and her daughter. In this dream and similar ones, the way in which I tried to solve the problem and in the process take it out on myself was to banish my personality, so I could no longer inflict harm on others.

The result was terror. I believe this type of dream is endemic to psychotic-like experience in general as patients of mine who have experienced psychotic breaks have had similar thoughts in the process of their recoveries.

And so, I bring these last issues up — the reaction of psychoanalysts to my presentation and my assertion that this was a psychotic break that had sequelae that gradually over years disappeared — as a final addendum to this recounting.

Footnotes

1. Ultimately, Darlene led a professionally successful, well-recognized, and apparently full life, unfortunately cut short by covid in 2021.

2. Your Mum and Dad. This film is online only as a trailer: https://mdb.com/title/tt11219876/

REFERENCES

American Psychiatric Association (2022): *Diagnostic and Statistical Manual of Mental Disorders (5th ed., text rev)*, Arlington, VA.

Bowers, M.B. (1974). *Retreat from sanity: the structure of emerging psychosis*. New York: Human Sciences Press.

Freud, S. (1901): The psychopathology of everyday life, *Standard Edition, 1*, 1–296.

—— (1911). Psycho-analytic notes upon an autobiographical account of a case of paranoia (dementia paranoides). *Standard Edition, 12*, 1–82.

—— (1924a). Neurosis and psychosis, *Standard Edition, 19*, 147–154.

—— (1924b). The loss of reality in neurosis and psychosis. In *Standard Edition, 19*, 181–188.

Hardin, H.T. (1985). On the vicissitudes of early primary surrogate mothering. *Journal of the American Psychoanalytic Association, 53*, 609–629

Hoffer, A (1971). Treatment of alcoholism with psychedelic therapy. In B. Aaronson and H. Osmond (Eds.) *Psychedelics: The uses and implications of hallucinogenic drugs*. Cambridge: Schenkman Publishing. pp. 357–366.

Loewald, H.W. (1960). On the therapeutic action of psycho-analysis. *International Journal of Psychoanalysis, 41*, 16–33.

Macalpine, I. & Hunter, R. (1955). *Daniel Schreber: Memoirs of my nervous illness.* London: William Dawson & Sons.

Reichbart, R. (2012). Presentation, *The Dynamics of a Psychosis: Up Close and Personal* in session entitled: *A Personal Account of Psychosis and Creativity* with Nancy McWilliams, Ph.D. as discussant (*Psychotic Experiences and Our Shared Humanity*) chaired by Robert Liss, Ph.D., Division 39, American Psychological Association, Santa Fe, New Mexico, April 20, 2012.

—— (2008). Screen memory: Its importance to object relations. *Journal of The American Psychoanalytic Association, 56,* 455–481.

—— (2019). *The paranormal surrounds us: Psychic phenomena in literature, culture and psychoanalysis.* Jefferson, NC: McFarland.

Acknowledgments

There are so many people who helped to make this book possible and I am sorry I can only enumerate the most prominent. For their analytic understanding and love: first and foremost, the psychoanalyst Jule Eisenbud, M.D. who played such a crucial part in this story and whose determination and insight changed my life forever; and then Joyce Steingart, Ph.D. who consolidated for me the discoveries of my first psychoanalysis with gentleness and patience. Both of them, now deceased, helped to plumb the depths of my personal history and psyche in ways that transformed me.

Then as part of my psychoanalytic education, the psycho-analysts Arlene Richards, Ed.D. and Janice Lieberman, Ph.D., and the psychologist Ruth Resch, Ph.D. all of whom taught me with such openness and insight: they never knew this story but the way in which they gave to me contributed to my ability to write it. Michael Moskowitz, Ph.D. has been a friend and colleague and I am grateful to him; and Robert Liss, J.D., Ph.D., who presided over my presentation at Division 39 in

85

New Mexico, has followed my career since high school and has been a presence that has provided welcome continuity. Sheldon Bach, Ph.D. in ways he did not know was a source of hope and inspiration. Most particularly, I cannot thank enough Nancy McWilliams, Ph.D. for her unstinting encouragement and her amazing scholarship; I am honored that she participated in the New Mexico presentation and now has so generously added the Foreword to this work.

The psychoanalytic atmosphere and the psychoanalytic members of three groups — the Institute for Psychoanalytic Training and Research (IPTAR) in New York City, the now defunct Psychoanalytic Society of New Jersey where I presented a version of this work, and the Black Psychoanalysts Speak organization — have contributed immeasurably to my understanding. And of course, I thank my patients who have helped me to apply what I learned to my clinical work and who have provided me with nuance and insight and love as they traversed their own adventures.

Personally, I thank those closest to me. I was fortunate in my parents and grandparents, although I depict them here with sometimes faults. Ultimately they were as wonderful as anyone could want. I do not mention this in this recounting, but my parents taught and practiced an enduring sense of social justice and fairness which made my choices possible, even when they did not entirely understand them. Paige Hooper-Reichbart was unstintingly supportive for many crucial years and taught me much. And then, most importantly, Nansie Ross, my significant other for over 30 years, has encouraged me, providing such reasonable guidance, and has never failed but to make me laugh. She has brought beauty, joy and love into my life which I hope I have been able to convey to the reader in the writing of this book.

www.ingramcontent.com/pod-product-compliance
Lightning Source LLC
Chambersburg PA
CBHW060246030426
42335CB00014B/1616